PROMISES

WORTH KEEPING

PROMISES FOR
SPIRITUAL GROWTH

MICHAEL Q. PINK

PROMISES WORTH KEEPING

ISBN 0529-10630-2

Written by:
Michael Q. Pink

Cover and book design by:
Herron/Largent Studios, Inc.
Atlanta, GA 30341

INTRODUCTION

As a child my father imparted his values of honesty, integrity and generosity. As a young man, I struggled to make these values mine and in the process I fell short of the mark. In 1985, God picked me up out of the miry pit, washed me clean and gave me another shot at life.

I knew that a good name was "more desirable than great wealth" (Proverbs 22:1) and I embarked on this new life with a goal of being a man of honor, who kept his promises. In January of 1986, I married an honorable woman, virtuous in every way who adhered to the highest standards of honor and together we made promises to God and to each other that have stood the test of time.

When I first heard the term "Promise Keeper" something inside of me leapt and the sound of those words resonated deep within me. It struck a chord of "honor" that I so deeply

INTRODUCTION

wanted to be identified with. I knew the book of Ecclesiastes, chapter five says that "it is better not to make a promise than to make one and not keep it." I knew for me and my house, a promise made would be a promise kept!

In life we make all kinds of promises, many of them without much thought or meaning. We promise to cut the lawn, pick up the paper and take out the garbage. We also promise to be faithful to our spouse, spend time with our children and take care of our health.

Promises made should be kept and in the pages of this book I trust you will find a thoughtful and meaningful collection of *promises worth keeping*.

—*Michael Pink*

For Brenda

God placed in me the seeds of honor,
but you have watered them with your words,
warmed them with your love and
with your very life, encouraged them to grow.

You are so fine to me!

1
to be my wife's best friend.

2
to pay people back with good
when they do evil to me.
(Matthew 5:44)

3
to stop and listen
when my children
tell me their dreams.

4
to shower my family with
random acts of kindness.

5
to be intimate and vulnerable
with my wife.

6
to seek to understand
what is the will of the Lord.

7

**to engage the imagination
of my children
through the gift of literature.**

8

**to be decisive even if it means
sometimes being wrong.**

9

**to commune with God
in my heart.**

10
to remember what it means
to be a child.

11
to pray earnestly
with thanksgiving.

12
even when it hurts to feel emotions,
I will allow myself to feel them anyway.

13
when the world is zigging, I will zag.

14
even when standing for what is right
means standing alone,
to still stand for what is right anyway.

15
to walk firm in the knowledge
that my past is redeemed, my present
makes sense and my future is secure.

16
to pray for those
who accuse me falsely that they
discover the goodness of God.

17
that when spring flowers
clothe the meadow,
to remember how much more
my heavenly Father will clothe me.
(Matthew 6:30)

18
to sow love into my wife's heart.

19
that when good enough
is good enough,
I will still do my best.

20
when the songbirds sing
their joyful song, to take notice
of the beauty of God's creation.

21
that when the storm clouds
gather against me,
to run to the rock of my salvation.
(Psalms 89:26)

22
that when the pressures of life
overwhelm me, I will remember
that he that is in me is greater
than he that is in the world.
(1 John 4:4)

23
that in the midst of my tough times,
I will not faint. (Proverbs 24:10)

24
to not be drunk with wine,
but be filled with the Spirit.
(Ephesians 5:18)

25
to remember that the Lord
will deliver me from affliction.
(Psalms 34:17)

26
to get up when I stumble or fall.
(Micah 7:8)

27
that when I suffer loss,
I will remember that I do not grieve
as those who have no hope.
(1 Thessalonians 4:13)

28
to overcome evil with good.
(Romans 12:21)

29
to have no fear when I walk through
the valley of the shadow of death.
(Psalms 23:4)

30
to draw strength from Christ
when the task looks impossible.
(Philippians 4:13)

31
to admit my need for love.

32
to not overestimate myself.

33
to keep a positive attitude
when trials and tribulations come,
because Christ has overcome the world.
(John 16:33)

34
to pray and be patient
during tribulation.

35
to bless those who curse me.
(Luke 6:28)

36
as much as is possible,
to live in peace with everyone.
(Romans 12:18)

37
to love sincerely, hating evil,
holding on to what is good.
(Romans 12:9)

38
to not take revenge on anyone.
Instead I will trust God to take care
of any wrong done to me.
(Romans 12:19)

39
when doing the right thing
means suffering loss,
I will still do
the right thing anyway.

40
as I become aware of my mistakes,
to not repeat them.

41
to thank God each morning
for the special attributes
of my spouse.

42
to plan spontaneous times
of recreation.

43
to hear when I listen.

44
to listen when I hear.

45
as I reflect on the day past,
to make it my goal to be able
to say, "time well spent."

46
to plan a weekend with my wife
where we can be alone
and rediscover our first love.

47
to honor my wife.
(1 Peter 3:7)

48
to honor my children by making
their special days special to me.

49
to live by faith and be powered by love.

50
to not look back, let up,
slow down or back away from
the purposes of God in my life.

51
to live life offensively,
planning strategically, enabled by grace
and governed by love.

52
to worship my God,
cherish my wife,
protect my family
and serve my fellow man.

53
to be guided by God's word,
inspired by his presence
and refreshed by his creation.

54
to walk patiently, pray courageously
and work valiantly.

55
that when I sit in the dark,
to allow the Lord to be my light.
(Micah 7:8)

56
to glorify God by completing
the work he gave me to do.
(John 17:4)

57
to take time for
meaningful conversation
with my children.

58
to listen to my spouse again,
for the first time.

59
to seek first to understand,
then to be understood.

60
to be finished with
low living, small planning,
colorless dreams and dwarfed goals.

61
to praise the small accomplishments
of my children.

62
to look for opportunities
in every adversity.

63
to sow love
where there is hatred.

64
to encourage my children
to discover the beauty
of God's creation.

65
to sing and make music
in my heart to the Lord.

66
to give thanks always for all things.

67
to find new ways to cherish my wife.

68
to invest in my children's
learning experience.

69
to never, never, never, give up.

70
to encourage my children
to discover the wonder of music.

71
to remember that
behind every dark cloud
is a golden sun.

72
to reconcile
whenever possible.

73
I will seek to understand cultures
different than my own.

74
to keep my promises
to my children.

75
at work to do more
than I'm paid for
and do it with excellence.

76
to sow peace
where there is turmoil.

77
when my enemy suffers loss,
I will not rejoice.
(Proverbs 24:17)

78
to make education interesting
to my children.

79
to walk in righteous paths.
(Psalms 23:3)

80
to search for wisdom with all my heart.
(Ecclessiates 7:25)

81
to increase my strength
by growing in knowledge.
(Proverbs 24:5)

82
to never abandon
the principles of mercy and truth.
(Proverbs 3:3)

83
to no longer seek position
or popularity to measure my value.

84
to trust in the Lord with all my heart
and not to lean on my own understanding.
(Proverbs 3:5)

85
to keep my promises
even when it hurts.
(Psalms 15:4)

86
to honor the Lord by giving
the first and best part of all my income.
(Proverbs 3:9)

87
to not reject the Lord's discipline.
(Proverbs 3:11)

88
to let the Lord be my confidence.
(Proverbs 3:26)

89
to not hold back anything good
from those who are entitled to it
if I have the power to do so.
(Proverbs 3:27)

90
to share my deepest feelings
with my wife.

91
to not argue with someone
for no reason.

92
to not envy or follow the example
of those who are violent.
(Proverbs 3:31)

93
to develop
a disciplined lifestyle.

94
to never abandon wisdom,
for it will watch over me
and protect me.
(Proverbs 4:6)

95
to guard my heart.
(Proverbs 4:23)

96
to sow understanding
where there is mistrust.

97
to tell the truth at all times.
(Colossians 3:9)

98
to live each day
as if it were my last,
because it might be.

99
to watch another sunset
with my wife.

100
to slow down the pace
when life starts to get hectic.

101
to be strengthened
by the faith I have received
and to overflow with thanksgiving.

102
to honor my children
by being with them on their birthday.

103
to not embarrass my children
by making fun of their mistakes.

104
to no longer seek promotion
by my peers or the praise of others
to determine my worth.

105
to hear the voice of God
in the silent roar of his creation.

I PROMISE . . .

106
to treasure those things which
I sometimes take for granted.

107
to be honest with God
at all times.

108
to remember that opportunities
are guarded by problems.

109
to live in a way
that honors God at all times.

110
to act like God is always with me
because he is.

111
to think thoughts
as though God were listening
because he is.

112
to see others the way Jesus does.

113
to worship God unashamedly
with all of my heart.

114
to thank God everyday
for the many ways
he has shown his love to me.

115
to cultivate a sense of deliberateness
in my worship of God.

116
to encourage my brother
when he falls, for fear that I fall myself.
(Galatians 6:1)

117
to be my brother's keeper.
(Genesis 4:9)

118
to love God with all my heart,
soul, mind and strength.
(Mark 12:30)

119
to spend time with the Lord
and get to know his heart.

120
to spend time learning God's ways
and knowing his will.

121
to share a hopeful word
with someone who is in despair.

122
to engage in daily,
life-changing prayer.

123
to offer myself as a living sacrifice,
completely acceptable to God.
(Romans 12:1)

124
to seek to know and understand
the feelings of my wife.

125
to get up one more time
than I'm knocked down.

126
to be merciful, even as
my Heavenly Father is merciful.
(Luke 6:36)

127
to fight for my family on my knees.

128
to keep myself from
being polluted by the world.
(James 1:27)

129
if my enemy is hungry, I will feed him.
If he is thirsty, I will give him a drink.
(Proverbs 25:21)

130
to conform my words to reality.
(honesty)

131
to conform reality to my words.
(integrity)

132
to speak in a way that
honors God and uplifts others.

133
to be an accurate reflection
of the person of Jesus Christ.

134
to value God's honor
above my reputation.

135
to be a man of my word.

136
to not be bought
or compromised.

137
to speak always
in the fear of the Lord

138
to be a lover of truth.

139
to let my words be kind
and well thought out.
(Colossians 4:6)

140
to not be detoured or lured away
by the glitter of this world.

141
to never cheat on my taxes
even if nobody would know.

142
to speak the truth in love.

143
that excellence will be
my trademark in all that I do.

144
to pursue vital relationships
with others for friendship,
accountability and support.

145
through my lifestyle
to demonstrate the reality
of Jesus Christ within me.

146
to no longer conform
to the pattern of this world.
(Romans 12:2)

147
to encourage my children
to explore the arts.

148
to acknowledge God
in all my ways
so he will direct my paths.

149
to walk worthy of the Lord,
fully pleasing him,
being fruitful in every good work
and growing in the knowledge of God.
(Colossians 1:10)

150
to continue in the faith,
not being moved
from the solid foundation
of the hope of the gospel.
(Colossians 1:23)

151
to watch less television.

152
to give my children
a healthy self-image.

153
to remember the source of my joy
in the midst of my sorrow.

154
to keep my mind on things above,
not on worldly things.
(Colossians 3:1)

155
to see the gentle side of strength
and the virtue of patience.

156
to let the word of Christ,
with all its wisdom
and richness, live in me.
(Colossians 3:16)

157
to read great books
and encourage my children
to do the same.

158
to allow no bitterness
to take root in my heart.

159
to live wisely,
making the most
of every opportunity.
(Ephesians 5:15, 16)

160
to complete the work
I have started.

161
to say what I mean
and mean what I say.

162
to exercise.

163
to take good care
of my physical body
so I can fulfill the purposes
God has for me.

164
to make good health
a lifestyle choice.

165
to exercise restraint
when indulgence is possible.

166
to help my children
discover their gifts and talents
and encourage them
in their development.

167
to make Jesus Christ central
to every decision in my life.

168
to drive like there
really is a tomorrow.

169
to put to death any sexual sin,
perversion, passion, lust
or greed that may be in me.
(Colossians 3:5)

170
to remember that there are
other passengers in the car
who may need to stop
more than every 400 miles
while driving to our vacation spot.

171
to attend my children's recitals,
plays and athletic events.

172
to let my children hear me
saying good things
about them to others.

173
to stop being critical of others.

174
to fulfill my vows to my spouse.

175
to expect excellence of effort,
not perfection of deed.

176
to sometimes let my children
win at the games we play.

177
to be the first
to initiate kindness
with my neighbor.

178
to live within our means.

179
to pay off the credit card
every month.

180
to no longer seek
to be first, right, best, rich or
famous to find fulfillment.

181
to stop using the credit card
when I can no longer afford
to pay it off every month.

182
to be transformed by the renewing
of my mind. (Romans 12:2)

183
to take responsibility for my future.

184
to forgive myself as
Christ has also forgiven me.

185
to return borrowed items
in better condition
than when I borrowed them.

186
to take time to teach my children
about God and his Son, Jesus Christ.

187
to treat others the way
I want to be treated.

188
to treat my wife like a queen
if I expect her to treat me like a king.

189
to love people and use things.

190
to give my wife a romantic card
just to say I love you.

191
to seek first God's kingdom
and his righteousness.
(Matthew 6:13)

192
to pursue a loving relationship
with the Creator, not the creation.

193
not to flinch
in the face of sacrifice.

194
to get firmly established
in my faith in Christ.
(Colossians 2:7)

195
to remember there is a God,
and I'm not him.

196
to cherish true friendship.

197
to forgive others
as Christ has forgiven me.
(Ephesians 4:32)

198
to be a good listener.

199
to be a faithful friend to my friends.

200
to keep private the things
told me in confidence.

201
to be faithful to my spouse.

202
to never make my wife the brunt of any joke.

203
to always publicly honor
and exalt my wife.

204
to never make fun of my children.

205
to take a walk on a regular basis.

206
to find a reason to be joyful today.

207
to thank others
for their acts of kindness.

208
to never give up on anyone.
Miracles happen.

209
to be a respecter of the laws
of my country.

210
to teach my children
the value of a work ethic.

211
to lead my family by example.

212
to refrain from profanity.
It demeans the human spirit.

213
to let my anger be Spirit controlled.

214
to take responsibility for my actions.

215
to be a good manager
of every thing God has given me.

216
to look for the opportunity
in the middle of every hardship.

217
to give, anonymously, to people in need.
(Matthew 6:4)

218
to be generous at all times.
(Proverbs 22:9)

219
to accept the help of others
with humility.

220
to live in such a way that
when my children think of fairness,
kindness and love they think of me.

221
that whatever I do will be done
wholeheartedly, as to the Lord.
(Colossians 3:23)

222
to model integrity
to my children.

223
to return the change that was
given to me in error at the store.

224
to examine my heart daily.

225
to come daily before my Father,
before I go anywhere else.

226
not to flinch in the face of adversity.

227
to never be so proud as to
not admit my mistakes.

228
to never use sarcasm.
Someone always gets hurt.

229
to let the peace of God
rule in my heart.
(Colossians 3:15)

230
to let people in front of me
when I'm stuck in traffic.

231
to be brave and very courageous
regardless of how I feel.

232
to affirm my children
after I discipline them.

233
to discover the gifts and talents
God has given me and use them.

234
to do the right thing
even when nobody notices.

235
to remember what is
special to my wife and freely give it
without her having to ask for it.

236
to inspire my children to go further
than I have gone.

237
to lead my family in prayer.

238
to tell the truth
regardless of the personal cost.

239
to believe the best about others.
(1 Corinthians 13:7)

240
to have hope in all things.
(1 Corinthians 13:7)

241
to love at all times.
(1 Corinthians 13:8)

242
to be the first to forgive.

243
to be the first to admit my wrong.

244
to love the unlovely.

245
to encourage the downcast.

246
to trust God at all times.

247
to influence my children more than
their strongest peer pressure.

I PROMISE . . .

248
to remember that my body
is the temple of the Holy Spirit.
(1 Corinthians 6:19)

249
not to negotiate with
the powers of darkness.

250
not to give the devil
any opportunity to work in my home.
(Ephesians 4:27)

PROMISES   WORTH   KEEPING

251
to be all that God
has purposed for me.

252
to be the kind of father
God wants me to be.

253
to remember that driving to work
was never intended to be
a competitive sport.

254
to be temperate in all things.

255
to not use my liberty for an excuse to sin.

256
to remember from where I have fallen.
(Revelation 2:5)

257
to love others when their sin
exceeds my own.

258
to not shoot the wounded.

259
to never risk my family's future
for my ambition.

260
to do a kind act to someone without
the person knowing it was me.

261
to write a nice letter to my pastor.

262
to plan happy surprises
for my children.

263
to deliberately build loving memories
for my children to cherish.

264
to allow crisis to bring our family
closer together.

265
to allow for the fact that
hurting people hurt people.

266
to be an agent of healing
for a hurting person.

267
to be a blessing
to someone else's life.

268
to get rid of my anger,
hot tempers, hatred, cursing,
obscene language and all similar sins.
(Ephesians 4:31)

269
to sow harmony
where there is discord.

270
to weep with those who weep.

271
to laugh with those who laugh.

272
to remember that sorrow
may endure for the night,
but joy comes in the morning.
(Psalms 30:5)

273
to bring my children little gifts
when they least expect it.

274
to keep on learning.

275
to lend, hoping for nothing in return.
(Luke 6:35)

276
to have big dreams,
but be faithful in small things.

277
to take responsibility for my finances.

278
to let my children know
how much I trust them
through my actions and my words.

279
to accentuate the positive attributes
in my children.

280
to never serve money
but to let it serve me.

281
to give to Caesar what is Caesar's
even if I don't like it.
(Mark 12:17)

282
to become like a child
in my trust of God.

283
to bring happiness
into the lives I touch.

284
to be a breath of fresh air
in a world of polluted values.

285
to monitor my dinner conversation
as if Christ were listening,
because He is.

286
to be a source of joy
to an unjoyful world.

287
to help my children exceed me
in every way.

288
to rejoice at my children's
every accomplishment.

289
to let my children know
how terrific I think they are.

290
to love my children
even when they disappoint me.

291
to love my wife
as Christ loves the church.
(Ephesians 5:25)

292
to pray intensely that I may stand mature
and complete in all the will of God.
(Colossians 4:12)

293
to love my children as
God the Father loves me.

294
to be long on forgiveness
and short on temper.

295
to not hesitate to swim
against the flow.

296
to measure my words before I speak.

297
to find out what's important
to my spouse.

298
not to accept mediocrity.

299
to notice and appreciate
the things of beauty God has made.

I PROMISE . . .

300
to be a guardian of the resources
God has put on this planet.

301
to hold material things lightly.

302
to read the Bible again,
for the first time.

303
to demonstrate my faith with works.

304
to match my works with faith.

305
to examine my heart often.

306
to question my motives honestly.

307
to write a love letter to my wife
on no special occasion.

308
to be a good manager
of the resources
God has given me.

309
to develop good habits
that will draw me closer to God.

310
not to give up or let up
until the Lord calls me home.

311
to treat my wife like a gift from God.

312
to respect my children's need for privacy.

313
to make my children feel significant.

314
to make my wife feel preferred
above all others.

I PROMISE . . .

315
to create an environment of love
and trust within my family.

316
to respect my wife's
need for security.

317
to take time to acknowledge
the daily acts of love done for me.

318
to learn the truth
about our history.

319
to learn what our spiritual forefathers
lived and died for.

320
to put aside foolish talk
and obscene jokes.
(Ephesians 5:4)

321
to learn what the early
fathers of the faith believed.

322
to leave a spiritual heritage for my children
and their children's children.

323
to leave judgment
and retaliation to God.
(Romans 12:19)

I PROMISE . . .

324
to let everything I say or do
be done in the name
of the Lord Jesus Christ.
(Colossians 3:17)

325
to uproot and be rid of
compromise from my life.

326
to have fun with my children.

327
to love my wife as my own body.

328
to practice doing the right things.

329
to do what I fear.

330
to step out of my comfort zone
and do something great.

I PROMISE . . .

331
to reduce conflict
by finding common goals.

332
to invest in my children.

333
to lay my life down for my wife.

334
to build on past victories.

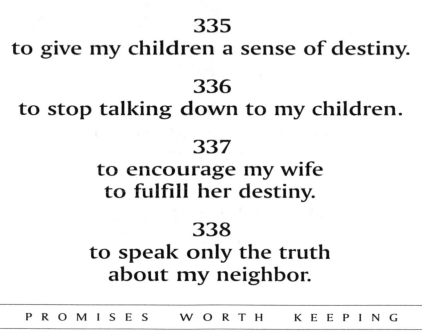

335
to give my children a sense of destiny.

336
to stop talking down to my children.

337
to encourage my wife
to fulfill her destiny.

338
to speak only the truth
about my neighbor.

339
to affirm the positive attributes
in my children.

340
to base my requests of others
in humility.

341
to walk humbly before my God.
(Micah 6:8)

342
to use my words to edify and encourage.

343
to let my children know
that I am personally committed
to their success.

344
to teach my children
their value is based on who they are,
not what they do.

345
to plan for the unexpected.

346
to let my children know
that I have confidence
that they will do the right thing.

347
to raise my expectations.

348
to build on small successes.

349
to encourage myself in the Lord.
(1 Samuel 30:6)

350
to remember that integrity
is a private victory
not an inherited trait.

351
to have worthy and achievable goals

352
to take the time to list all
that God has given me to take care of.

353
to enjoy my children
while they are young.

354
to gain encouragement
from people who have faith in God.

355
to comfort others with the comfort
I have received from God.
(2 Corinthians 1:4)

356
to obligate myself to succeed
with my family relationships.

357
to nurture hope in those
who are fragile and weak.

358
to set a higher standard
than the world sets for me.

359
to make my attitude reflect
my desired result.

360
to be thankful in adversity.

361
to pay my bills on time.

I PROMISE . . .

362
to remember the poor.
(Galatians 2:10)

363
to celebrate the uniqueness
of each of my children.

364
to send flowers to my wife
and take the time to smell them.

365
to be a man of principle.

366
to encourage my family
to have a meaningful relationship
with Jesus Christ.

367
to hold faithfulness and integrity
as first principles.

368
to hold myself responsible
for a higher standard
than anyone else expects.

369
to hold important principles
as inflexible.

370
to prepare my children for the storms,
for they will surely come.

371
to secure the good of others
and my good will be secured.

372
to reply kindly to angry people.
(Proverbs 15:1)

373
to pursue God
and let riches pursue me.
(Matthew 6:33)

374
to teach my children to see
the positive side
of negative circumstances.

375
to let a wise person mentor me.

376
to be a mentor to my children.

377
to begin with the end in mind.

378
to remember that quality
begets quantity.

379
to remember that
practice makes permanent,
not perfect.

380
to remember that chance
favors the prepared.

382
to never promise more
than I can perform.

383
to never use two words
when one will do.

384
to be renewed
in the spirit of my mind.
(Ephesians 4:23)

385
to allow my children to make mistakes.

381
to cultivate an attitude of gratitude.

386
to prepare for the opportunities
that will surely come.

387
to do common things
with uncommon excellence.

388
to remember that everything
under heaven has a purpose.

389
to remember
where purpose is unknown,
abuse is inevitable.

390
to think noble thoughts
and take noble actions.

391
to always be willing
to learn from others,
even my children.

392
to faithfully carry out
all of my current responsibilities.

392
to seize the opportunity
in every difficulty.

393
to not expect the thrill of victory
apart from the pain of adversity.

394
to make sure the things
that matter most are never at the mercy
of things which matter least.

395
to live strategically, plan thoughtfully
and expect the best.

396
to profit from my mistakes
and try again.

397
to walk courageously
where others fear to tread.

398
to labor to enter into rest.
(Hebrews 4:11)

I PROMISE . . .

399
to be true to myself.

400
to pray for wisdom and courage
above things and circumstances.

401
to be of firm resolve
but have a gentle heart.

402
to take responsibility for my health.

403
to not be afraid
to go against the grain.

404
to be wise as a serpent
and harmless as a dove.
(Matthew 10:16)

405
to be punctual
as a matter of principle.

406
to be an ambassador of Jesus Christ
wherever I go.

407
to avoid the path to temptation.

408
to live this life by faith
in the Son of God, who loved me
and gave himself for me.
(Galatians 2:20)

409
to not try to complete
by my own strength that which
was begun in the Spirit.
(Galatians 3:3)

410
to please God instead of people.

411
to remember that in Christ Jesus
there is no more race, class or gender.
(Galatians 3:28)

412
to stand firm in the freedom
Christ won for me.

413
to love my neighbor as myself.
(Matthew 22:39)

414
to walk in the Spirit so as
not to fulfill the lust of the flesh.
(Galatians 5:16)

415
to restore others when they fall.
(Galatians 6:1)

416
to affirm my children privately,
publicly and often.

417
to not think too highly of myself.

418
to bear others burdens
and so fulfill the law of Christ.
(Galatians 6:2)

419
to do good to all
at every opportunity, especially
to my Christian brothers and sisters.

420
to not grow tired of doing what is right.

421
to remember that the sun is
always shining—even at night.

421
to understand the pain of other races
and work to heal it.

423
to develop the habit of intimacy
with God.

424
to take time to rejuvenate.

425
to be vulnerable with my wife.

426
to learn my wife's idea
of a romantic evening.

427
to plan romantic evenings
with my wife.

428
to answer my children's
questions truthfully.

429
to find out how
my children spell love.
(t-i-m-e)

430
to listen to my children's dreams.

431
to look for ways to build confidence
in my children.

432
to give my family the best of me,
not the best of things.

433
to instill respect for the elderly
in my children.

434
to leave my grudges
at the foot of the cross.

435
to find work that is consistent
with my talents.

436
to try and out-serve my spouse
in our marriage.

437
to move forward toward the goal
to win the prize that God offers.

438
to start each day
on a note of praise to my God.

439
to never let a day go by
that my children don't know
I love them.

I PROMISE . . .

440
to search for the wealth of God's kingdom,
hidden in each of us

441
to magnify the Lord, not the problem.

442
to exalt the message, not the messenger.

443
to become friends with someone
of a different cultural heritage.

444
to teach my children
financial principles
while they are young.

445
to go confidently to
God's throne of kindness
in my time of need.

446
to be kind to others,
sympathetic and forgiving.

447
to imitate God
since I am His child.

448
to learn the things
that please the Lord.

449
to redeem the time,
because the days are evil.
(Ephesians 5:16)

450
to work like God is my boss,
because He is!
(Colossians 4:1)

451
to place myself under the authority
of others out of respect for Christ.

452
to honor my father and mother.
(Exodus 20:12)

453
to not provoke my children
and make them bitter.
(Ephesians 6:4)

454
to raise my children in Christian training
and instruction. (Ephesians 6:4)

455
to be strong in the Lord
and be mighty in His strength.
(Ephesians 6:10)

456
to do the will of God from my heart.
(Ephesians 6:6)

457
to serve my employer as if
I were serving Jesus Christ, because I am.
(Colossians 3:23)

458
to catch my children doing
something good and praise them.

459
to put on all the armor
that God supplies and take a stand
against the devil's strategies.
(Ephesians 6:11)

460
to remember that my fight
is not with flesh and blood,
but against wicked spiritual forces.
(Ephesians 6:12)

461
to overcome all obstacles
and stand my ground.
(Ephesians 6:13)

462
to take vacations with my family.

463
to not be ashamed
of the gospel of Jesus Christ.
(Romans 1:16)

464
to be a cheerful giver.
(2 Corinthians 9:7)

465
to pray in the Spirit in every situation,
using every kind of prayer
and request there is.
(Ephesians 6:18)

466
not to gossip.
(Proverbs 26:20)

467
to go the extra mile.

468
to do more than is expected
of me on the job.

469
to not slander the person
who signs my paycheck.

470
to take my wife out for dinner
for no reason at all.

471
to gather regularly with
other believers.

472
to pursue the true riches
of God's kingdom.

473
to choose my television programs
as if Christ were with me,
because He is.

474
to keep my expectations high
and my expenses low.

475
to grow through my pain.

476
to admit my need for help.

477
to think and act like a child of God.

478
to be trustworthy.

479
to be the father my children need.